NO-SWEAT SCIENCE™ OPTICAL ILLUSION EXPERIMENTS

Michael A. DiSpezio

Illustrated by Dave Garbot

Sterling Publishing Co., Inc.
New York

Somewhere, long ago, in a universe called Brooklyn, my passion for science was nurtured and shaped by artists of the classroom. I dedicate this book to these science teachers: Mrs. Ackerman (7th and 8th grade science), Mr. Schecter (H.S. biology), Mr. Pollack (advanced H.S. biology), Mr. Neuman (H.S. physics), Dr. Levin (invertebrate zoology), Dr. Franz (marine ecology), and Dr. Harris (marine geology). I'd like to recognize the kid-friendly artistic talents of this series's artist, Frances Zweifel. I'd also like to acknowledge the friendship, literary skills, and time invested in this project by my editor, Hazel Chan.

Library of Congress Cataloging-in-Publication Data

Dispezio, Michael A.
  No sweat science : optical illusion experiments / Michael A. Dispezio ; illustrated by Dave Garbot.
       p. cm. -- (No sweat science)
    Includes index.
  Previously published: Simple optical illusion experiments with everyday materials. New York : Sterling Pub., c2000.
    ISBN-13: 978-1-4027-2336-0
    ISBN-10: 1-4027-2336-9
  1. Optical illusions--Juvenile literature. [1. Optical illusions--Experiments. 2. Experiments.] I. Garbot, Dave, ill. II. Dispezio, Michael A. Simple optical illusion experiments with everyday materials. III. Title.

QP495.D575 2007
152.14'8--dc22
                                        2007009210

10 9 8 7 6 5 4 3 2 1

Published by Sterling Publishing Co., Inc.
387 Park Avenue South, New York, NY 10016
© 2007 by Sterling Publishing Co., Inc.
Previously published as *Simple Optical Illusion Experiments with Everyday Materials*
© 2000 by Michael A. DiSpezio
Distributed in Canada by Sterling Publishing
c/o Canadian Manda Group, 165 Dufferin Street,
Toronto, Ontario, Canada M6K 3H6
Distributed in the United Kingdom by GMC Distribution Services,
Castle Place, 166 High Street, Lewes, East Sussex, England BN7 1XU
Distributed in Australia by Capricorn Link (Australia) Pty. Ltd.
P.O. Box 704, Windsor, NSW 2756, Australia

Sterling ISBN-13: 978-1-4027-2336-0
        ISBN-10: 1-4027-2336-9

For information about custom editions, special sales, premium and corporate purchases, please contact Sterling Special Sales Department at 800-805-5489 or specialsales@sterlingpub.com.

CONTENTS

Before You Begin 5
Bee Smart/Be Safe 7

Sticking Around (Illusions of Motion) 8
Lasting Thoughts • Happy Trails • Fan Trails • Beamer
• Light the Candle • More Spun Fun • Shoebox
Spinner • Flights of Imagination • Flappin' Without a
Flipper • Slot Shot • Assemble Your Own Flip Book
• Flippin' Fin Fun • Stencil the Snail • Twists and
Turns • A Cast of Two

Eye Tricks (Hardwired Illusions) 42
Blind Spot • Where Have All the Colors Gone? • Where
Did You Get Those Shades? • Field Trip • More
Fieldwork • Pump Up the Difference • Not Fade Away
• Color Code • Pink Pigs • Balancing Act • A Different
Spin on Color Perception • Colors in Black and White

Stretching The Truth
(Distortions of Length and Size) 66
Illusionary Lengths • Room for Mistakes • Tracks of the
Trade • Adding Arrowheads • Rulers Don't Lie . . .
Right? • Coining an Illusion • More Coinage • Tricky
Trapezoids

Tilts, Twists, and Topsy-Turvies
(Jumble of Bumble) 85
A New Slant on Things • Bending In • Warp Speed
• Upside Downside • Arch Enemy • Ruler
Interference • Setting a Side Aside • Comparing Colors
• Imaginary Square • Mosaic Madness

Fantastic Flat-Screen Phantoms
(Illusions of Depth) 102
Dominant View • Come Together • Handy Hole-in-One
• Stereo Pairs • Free Viewing • Two-Level Float
• Wallpaper • Seeing Red . . . and Blue • Making
Targets • A Smooth Transition • 3-D Cube

Index 125

BEFORE YOU BEGIN

Look down the street. What do you see? Is the scene in color? Does it appear as a flat image, like a picture, or is there something more? Do the people and cars separate from the background? Do faraway objects look like they are part of a tiny world, or are they seen as regular-sized objects that are far off?

The ability to see and to understand what you see depends upon both biology and experience. By biology, we mean your eye, optic nerve, and the incredible system of nerve cells that make up the part of your brain that gathers up what you see.

Understanding what you see also depends upon your experiences. You continuously collect a record of things you've seen. You store and perfect gathering tricks that are used to make sense of what your eyes

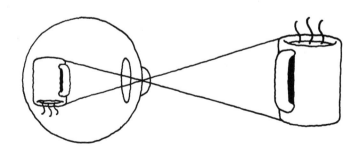

detect—otherwise it would be too much for your sense of sight to gather again all the things you've seen before as it sorts through extra and unfamiliar sights.

Most of the time these shortcuts work. They create a correct view of your real world. These tricks separate objects close to you from those farther away and keep them in their correct shape, size, and color.

But what if the shortcuts don't work? What if something gets in the way and somehow what you see goes down the wrong information route in your brain? What happens then? The result is a case of mistaken identity called an optical illusion.

An optical illusion is something that appears differently from what it actually is; some can make things look darker, lighter, wider, bigger, straighter, rounder, higher, or lower.

Other types of viewing tricks can make objects pop out as if they're going to touch you. And others can create the appearance of smooth motion from quickly flipping a stack of paper. The list goes on and on, but instead of reading about these tricks, why not construct them?

Many of the experiments in this book begin with an optical trick you might have seen before. Then, using simple materials, you get the chance to experiment with this illusion. You'll use what you've uncovered to better understand the science and "magic" of the experience.

Once you've made the basic illusion, you'll often be challenged to increase your understanding. There are questions to help get you started. But remember, these questions are only meant as a starting point from which to "explore" on your own. The real questions will come from your understanding, playfulness, and passion to learn.

So why just read about all this amazing stuff? Let's jump into your journey of optical illusion science!

Bee Smart/Be Safe

Using common sense is your most powerful tool to doing safe experiments. If an activity seems as if it might be unsafe, have an adult help you. Also, follow these general rules:

1. Protect your eyes! Never bring any sharp objects close to them.
2. When looking through rolled paper tubes, cover the end that you'll be looking through with your hands before bringing it to your eye.
3. Finish reading through the "What to do" instructions before you start. This read-through not only will help you find any safety concerns, it will also give you a thorough idea of what you'll be doing.
4. If a step needs you to cut or punch holes, ask an adult to help you do this.
5. Never look directly at the sun (or any other very bright object).
6. Do not use any laser lights in any of these experiments.
7. Be careful when working with scissors, sharp edges, and pushpins.
8. Use only an AA cell when making your electrical circuits. DO NOT use the AC electricity that comes from a wall outlet.

 The safety bee will appear throughout the book as a reminder.

STICKING AROUND: ILLUSIONS OF MOTION

Even though you weren't aware of it, your brain was very confused by the last TV show you saw. Does this sound strange? Perhaps, but no stranger than making the illusion of smooth motion from a stack of flip book pages.

Your brain is an impressive piece of machinery. Like a computer, it can do all sorts of tasks. Most of the time it can successfully deal with an incredible amount of information. However, when too much is presented, your brain applies shortcuts to deal with this excess. This frees up the brain to concentrate on the important things.

Suppose someone shows you two pictures of a bird: one with its wings stretched out and one with its wings held against its body. Most likely you will see and remember two separate images.

Suppose they quickly replace one image with another. No problem. If they replace it slowly, you'll still see two separate images. Now let's speed this up so that the images flip back and forth to about twenty

images in a second. At that rate, a confusing amount of information reaches your brain. It can't deal with seeing twenty separate images in a second. There is way too much information. As a result, your brain gets tricked into creating an illusion of smooth motion that seems to fill the gaps between the images. That's the basic rule of movies, videos, and flip books.

You can see these separate images on a length of movie film. They're called frames. If you examine this plastic film closely, you'll notice that each frame is slightly different from the one before and the one after it (unless, of course, there is no motion occurring). When these frames are shown on the screen of a movie theater, the illusion of smooth motion is created.

But what about videotape? Where are the frames in this type of motion? Good question. The frames are there, but they are recorded as magnetic signals in the tape material. If you have a VCR that can show frame-by-frame action, you can see each of the frames. Like the projector in a movie theater, the VCR shows these separate images at a fast enough rate to create the illusion of smooth and continuous motion.

Lasting Thoughts

Can you keep an image in your mind? You bet you can. The fancy term for this ability is *persistence of vision*. Suppose you are looking at an object and it disappears. For a short time, an image of that object remains in the brain. Although it stays for only a fraction of a second, this period is long enough to form the foundation for motion illusions.

You need:

white or light-colored checker piece
black marker

What to do:

First, make sure that no one will be upset if you mark up the white checker piece. If that isn't a problem, use your marker and draw a spot in the middle on one side of the checker piece. On the other side, draw a thick ring along its edge. Wait until the marks dry.

Stand the checker piece between the thumb of one hand and the index finger of the other hand. Make the checker spin by quickly pulling your fingers away. At disk level, look at the spinning pattern. What do you see?

What happens:

As the disk spins, the marks blend together and form a ghostlike pattern. This pattern has both the center spot and the thick ring along its edge.

Why:

As the disk spins, your eyes see both patterns. Here's where persistence of vision enters the picture (and stays). Since the spin is quick, the image from one side of the chip doesn't have enough time to fade before the next pattern appears. Your brain keeps both images and blends them into one image of a spot inside a circle.

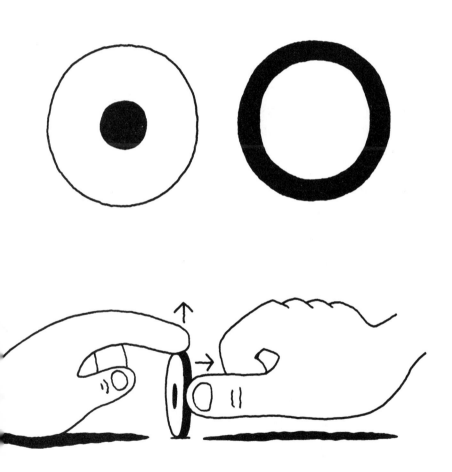

Happy Trails

Have you ever gone to a laser light show? If so, you were probably treated to a great show of images made by beams of laser light. As these beams swept back and forth, they made lasting outlines of familiar objects.

You need:
flashlight
dark room with a mirror

CAUTION: Do not use a laser light instead of a flashlight in this experiment.

Right light!

What to do:
Switch on the flashlight. Enter the room and make it as dark as possible. Stand in front of the mirror. Quickly

shake the flashlight back and forth. While the beam moves, look into the mirror at the shining end of the flashlight. What do you see?

Now quickly rotate the flashlight in small circles. What do you see now? Can you move the beam to form the outline of a familiar shape?

What happens:

The beam of the flashlight creates what appears to be a continuous trail of light.

Why:

The quick movements retrace the beam's position before the lasting image has time to disappear. This creates a trace that appears to be a continuous trail of light.

Fan Trails

Imagine an aircraft's propeller. When the propeller isn't moving, there is no illusion. However, when the aircraft's screw begins to rotate, the propeller sweeps out a circle of persistent image.

You need:
paper
marker

What to do:
Roll the paper into a tight roll. Use the marker to draw a thin line across the center of the paper. Holding one end of the roll, quickly fan the paper back and forth. Examine the arc created by the sweep. What do you see?

What happens:

At a fast enough speed, the paper and mark make a clear arc.

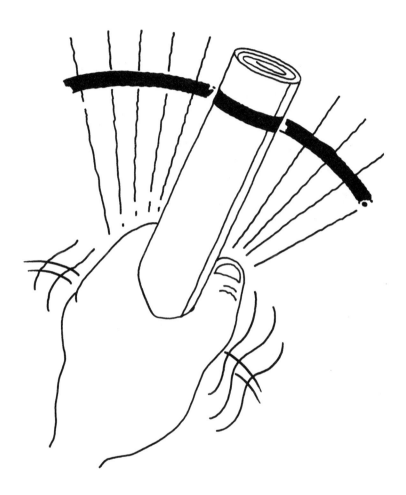

Why:

A fast sweep creates a ghostlike arc. The unmarked part of the paper produces a light, mostly see-through blur. The marked line creates a dark and clear curve.

Beamer

Switch on a movie projector. Its beam of light races across the theater and strikes the screen in front of you. The image appears on the screen. But were you aware that a blurred copy of this image is found all along the route between the projector and screen? It's there, yet you don't see it.

You need:

flashlight
hand lens
clay
tape
pencil
35mm slide

What to do:

Tape the 35mm slide to the lens of the flashlight. Place this "projector" on top of a table so that its beam points to a nearby wall. Move the flashlight back from the table's edge. Switch on the flashlight and look at the blurred image shown on the wall.

To focus this image, you'll need to put a hand lens in front of the slide. Keeping the beam aimed at the lens, move the hand lens back and forth along the tabletop until the image is in focus. Keep the lens in place by putting its handle into a lump of clay that is stuck to the table.

Hold one end of the pencil. Place its free end into the projected beam between the wall and the hand lens. Shake your wrist quickly back and forth as if you are fanning the pencil in the beam. What do you see?

What happens:

The entire projected image appears on the moving pencil.

Why:

Persistence of vision. As the pencil moves through the beam, a slice of the projected image falls on it. Before this image leaves your brain, the rest of the image is cast onto the pencil. Since the pencil is moving quickly, an entire picture stays before any of it is dropped from your memory. Your brain does the rest to combine the continuous view into a single, complete image.

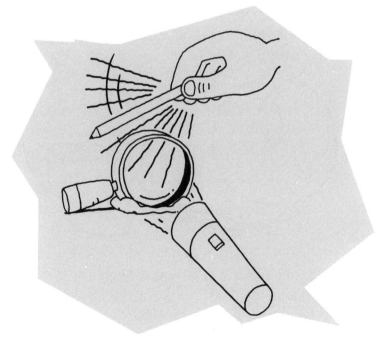

Light the Candle

In the early 1800s, inventors created fun uses for the persistence of vision. One of their simplest inventions was a toy called the *thaumatrope,* which means "spinning marvel." Was it really marvelous? You be the judge.

You need:

stapler   scissors
kite string   tape
index card (or heavy paper stock)

What to do:

Cut out two disks from the index card. The disks should be about the same size as the ones shown below. Copy the drawing of the flame onto one of the disks. Copy the candle onto the other disk. Use the illustrations below as a guide.

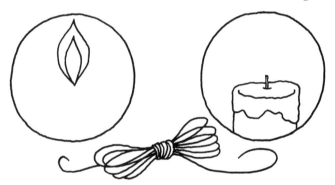

Using the scissors, carefully cut a section of kite string about 6 inches (15.2 cm) in length.

Flip one of the disks over so that its blank side faces up. Put the string in the center of the disk (see illustration

1). Make sure that the string is the same length in both directions. Tape the string to the disk.

Make a "sandwich" using the other disk. Be sure that both pictures face outward and one is upside down. Use a stapler to keep the disks together (illustration 2).

Hold a section of string in each hand. Twist the string back and forth so that the disks spin. Look at the image on the disks (illustration 3).

What happens:

The flame appears on the wick of the candle.

Why:

Here is another example of persistence of vision at work. As the disks spin, you see images of both the flame and candle. Since they flash at a very fast rate, each image stays while the other is shown. Your brain combines both images to create the burning candle.

More Spun Fun

Now that you know how to construct a spinning marvel, here's an assortment of thaumatropical drawings. Blending them together is as easy as lighting a candle. And for more spun fun, create your own drawings!

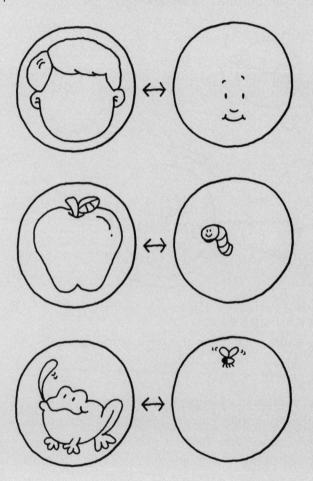

Shoebox Spinner

Now that you know how a thaumatrope works, why not build a permanent spinner in a box?

You need:

narrow shoebox
pushpin
stapler

scissors
heavy-stock paper
long pencil with point

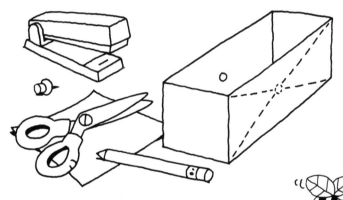

SAFETY NOTE: Young experimenters will need the help of an adult when using the pushpin and pencil to poke holes in the shoebox.

Sharp points!

What to do:

Find the center of the long side of the shoebox. Use the pushpin to carefully poke a hole at this point. Continue poking along the edge of the hole to make it bigger. Then insert and twist the pointed end of a pencil into this opening. The final hole should be large enough to allow the pencil to spin freely without getting stuck to the box. Repeat these steps to create a hole on the opposite side of the box.

Photocopy or trace each of the drawings below onto two separate sheets of heavy-stock paper. Use your scissors to cut out each square.

Put these pictures around the center of a pencil. Make sure one is upside down. Staple these pictures together. Make sure that the stapled sleeve doesn't slip when the pencil is spinning. Carefully slide the completed sleeve off the pencil.

Insert the pencil into one of the box holes. Slip the sleeve over the pencil part that is now in the box. Slide this sleeve along the pencil as you move the pencil across the box. Put the free end of the pencil in the other box hole.

Look down into the box and spin the pencil.

What happens:
The frog appears on the lily pad.

Why:
Before your brain has the chance to "dump" the image of the frog, the image of the lily pad appears. Since both images are in the brain at the same time, you put them together and make a combined image of both drawings.

What if the pictures of the frog and lily pad are stapled together, both images right side up? Will this change the effect? What might you see? Make a guess, then experiment to find out if you are right!

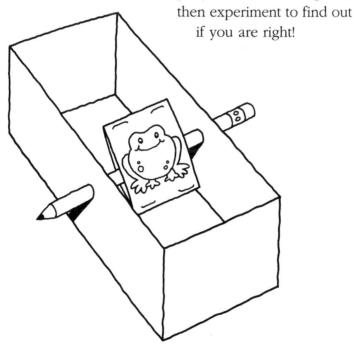

Flights of Imagination

Imagine looking at two pictures of a balloon. One image shows the balloon flat without any air. The other shows the balloon full of air. Close your eyes. Can you see the balloon as it becomes full? Most likely you can. From experience, you remember what a balloon looks like as it fills with air.

For this experiment, you'll discover how your brain can fill in the "gaps" between two different images.

You need:

pencil	scissors
tape	heavy-stock paper

What to do:

Photocopy or copy the two drawings of this bird onto a sheet of heavy-stock paper. Use your scissors to carefully cut along the rectangular edge. Fold the rectangle in half along the dotted line. Make sure that the images face outward. Use tape to keep this sleeve together and slip it over a pencil. Use tape to keep it in place.

Place the free end of the pencil between your palms. Practice rubbing your hands together so that the image flips back and forth. In order to get the best effect, you'll have to rub the pencil so that each of the two images appears straight-on at the end of each hand movement.

As the image flips back and forth, what do you see? Does your brain fill in any gaps? Does changing the speed of the flip do anything to the illusion?

What happens:

When you flip the image at the right speed, the bird's wings appear to flap with smooth and continuous up-and-down motion.

Why:

This experiment brings a new idea: *key frame*. A key frame is an image that shows the beginning or end of a movement. In this case, we have two key frames. One key frame shows the bird's wings at the top of the stroke. The other image shows the bird's wings at the bottom of the stroke.

When the sleeve spins at a fast enough rate, your brain locks on to these two key images. Not only do the wings' positions stay in your mind, but they tell you where the motion begins and ends. Your brain does the rest. It fills in the missing action with the most likely positions of the wings so that the bird appears to be flying!

Flappin' Without a Flipper

Here's another simple tool that can create the illusion of motion between two key frames.

You need:

paper

scissors

marker

pencil

What to do:

Cut out a strip of paper about 8 inches x 3 inches (20.3 cm x 7.6 cm). Fold the strip lengthwise to form a 4-inch x 3-inch (10.2 cm x 7.6 cm) booklet. Hold the booklet so that the crease is at the top.

On the top "cover," draw a simple bird. The bird's wings should be up. Fold back the cover. On the bottom page, draw an image of the bird with its wings down. Be sure that you draw the bottom image *directly* below the top image so that the two images line up.

Fold down the cover and wrap it up and around a pencil. Remove the pencil. Notice that the paper now curls. Place the

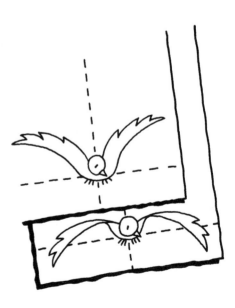

pencil back on the curl. As you move the pencil back and forth, the curled paper will cover and show the lower image. See what happens to the bird when you move the pencil at a fast enough rate.

What happens:

The wings appear to beat with a continuous, but sometimes jerky, motion.

Why:

By moving the pages fast enough, one key frame stays in your mind as the other is shown. Your brain does the rest. To understand these frames, your eyes and brain fill in the difference in the key frames to create the illusion of motion.

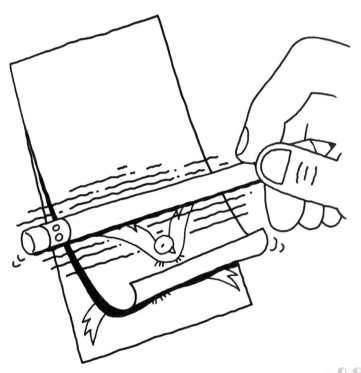

Slot Shot

Animators, people who draw cartoons, work with key frames. They often create the key frames and then give them to their assistants. The assistants could be either computers or people. The human helpers are known as "in-betweeners."

You need:

  heavy-stock paper
  scissors
  ruler
  markers
  tape

What to do:
Cut a sheet of $8^{1}/_{2}$ inch x 11 inch heavy-stock paper in half widthwise. You'll use just one of these halves ($8^{1}/_{2}$ inches x $5^{1}/_{2}$ inches) to make the viewer.

Fold and heavily crease one of these pieces in half widthwise. Tape the two edges that meet. This will make a flat cardboard sleeve ($4^{1}/_{4}$ inches x $5^{1}/_{2}$ inches).

Now you need to create a series of slots that are equally spaced and go about three-fourths up the side of the viewer. Start at the left end and mark off twelve vertical lines across the viewer sleeve. These lines should be about 3/8 inch (1 cm) apart. You'll see that this will leave a wider slot on the right end of the viewer. This is where you'll be holding on to the viewer.

Leaving the right edge alone, cut the lines you've drawn. Then bend every other slot away from the viewer and use the scissors to cut it out.

Photocopy or cut out the image of the insect (see page 30) onto a sheet of heavy-stock paper. Trim the paper so that it fits within the viewer.

When you put the sheet into the viewer, notice how the slotted pattern of the insect lets only one image

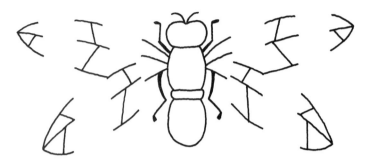

show at a time. Now quickly move the pattern into and out of the sleeve. What do you see?

What happens:

At the right speed, the insect's wings get a "filled-in" back-and-forth motion.

Why:

The viewer lets only one key frame show through at a time. As you move the insect image back and forth, both key frames are displayed. At a fast enough rate, one of the images stays in your mind as the other is seen. Your brain does the rest and fills in the in-between action.

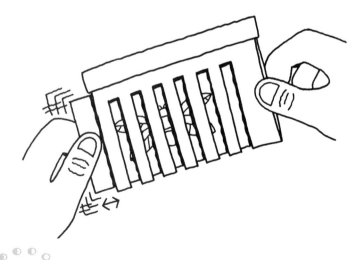

Assemble Your Own Flip Book

In the following four experiments, you'll be creating illusions on the pages of flip books. By using your thumb to quickly flip the pages of frames you've drawn, you'll have your own animation scenes.

To save money and trips to the supply store, you can assemble your own flip books from scrap and reusable materials. All you need are pieces of scrap paper, a pair of scissors (for trimming), and a binder clip.

First, get a stack of twenty to fifty sheets of scrap paper. Trim the paper so that the pages are all about the same size. Tap the stack on the table so that the bottom edges are in line. Place a binder clip over the top, and less even, end. Presto! You have a blank animation book.

You can create your illusions on the corners, bottom, and side edges of this stack. When there's no more space, flip it upside down and use the clean sides. After you're done with the flip book, throw out the paper but save the binder clip for making more flip books.

Flippin' Fin Fun

Flip, flip, flip, flip, flip. Have you ever made flip book animations? If so, then you'll recall having taken a simple motion and broken it down into its small steps. Each step was drawn on a separate sheet of paper. When this stack of images was flipped at a fast enough rate, you created the illusion of motion. Now that you know some of its science, why not do this again?

You need:

small writing pad (or your homemade flip book stack)
pencil

What to do:

For this first flip book, we'll start out with a very simple subject: a shark fin. Since the fin and water surface are easy to draw, we won't use a stencil.

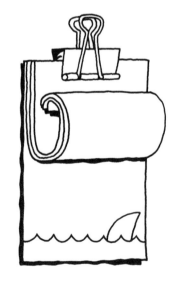

On the last page of your blank pad, draw the fin and water at the lower right corner of the page. That's it. This frame is complete.

Lower the next page. On this sheet, draw the same fin and water. This time, make sure that your drawing is placed just slightly to the left of the first image. "Just slightly" means about the width of a toothpick or thickness of the wire used to make paper clips.

Lower the next page and redraw the image. Again, move the image a toothpick's width to the left.

Keep redrawing this image on the remaining sheets until the shark has swum off the screen.

Now it's time for some action. Bend up the stack of pages. Release them so that the pages fall at a quick and steady pace. What happens when you flip the pages?

What happens:

The shark appears to swim across the page.

Why:

Persistence of vision is at work again. Before your brain can "dump" the previous position of the shark fin, a new one appears. Your brain creates the illusion of a smooth movement from one image to the next. The result is an illusion of continuous, but sometimes jerky, motion.

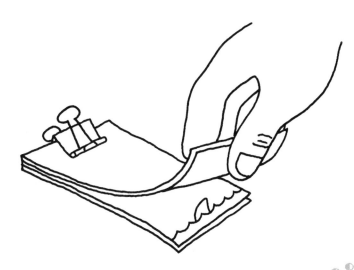

Stencil the Snail

The subject of this animation is a little bit harder to draw: it's a snail. However, to keep things easy (and make sure that the snail remains a snail), you're going to trace copies of the image onto the pages of your flip book.

You need:

pencil   scissors

snail stencil

small writing pad (or your homemade flip book stack)

What to do:

Photocopy or cut out this picture of the snail. It will be used as a stencil to trace the same image into your flip book. Keep a thin border around the snail when you cut it out.

Turn to the last page of your flip book. First, we need to make sure that the stenciling will work. Insert the snail stencil just beneath the page. The snail's dark outline should show through the white paper. If it doesn't, you'll need to use thinner paper.

Place the stencil so that only the snail's antenna is beneath the page. Trace this part of the snail onto the page. Don't worry about the rest of the body. Remove the snail stencil.

Lower the next page. Place the stencil beneath this blank page. Place the snail about a toothpick's width farther onto the page. Draw this second image.

Lower the next page. Insert the stencil beneath it and move the snail another toothpick's distance onto the page. Draw this image.

Continue inserting, moving, and drawing the image of the snail until it has crawled off the page.

Flip the stack and see how the image of the snail moves across the paper in a continuous and smooth motion.

What happens:
The snail slithers onto, across, and off the page.

Why:
Persistence of vision. Need we say more?

Twists and Turns

So far, our animated characters have moved straight across your paper stage. Here's your chance to add a slight twist and turn to that motion.

You need:
small writing pad (or your homemade flip book stack)
pencil

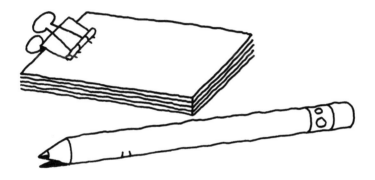

What to do:
Since you already know how to do this, we'll keep it simple and short. Turn to the last page of your flip book.

Draw an image of a fly in the bottom right corner of the page.

Lower the next page. Draw another fly image slightly to the left. Remember that to create a smooth motion, each drawing of the fly should be about the width of a toothpick away.

Lower the next page. Draw another fly image. This time, start curving the path upward.

As you continue drawing the images, make a path in which the fly completes a circular turn. When its turn finishes, have the fly buzz off the page.

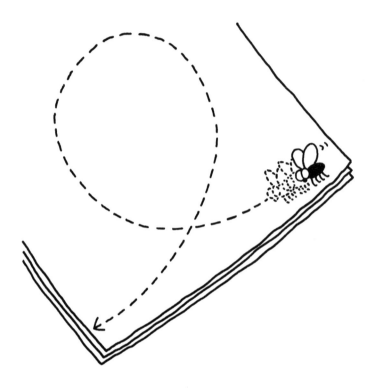

What happens:
This time, your animated character follows a circular path before heading off the page.

Why:
Persistence of vision creates the illusion of smooth motions along a circular path.

A Cast of Two

Our last animation is a bit more difficult. It uses two stencils to make a chase scene.

You need:

    small writing pad (or your homemade flip book stack)
    pencil
    scissors
    small fish stencil
    larger fish stencil

What to do:

Photocopy or cut out the picture of both fish. They will be used as stencils to trace the same images across the pages of your flip book. Keep a thin frame around both stencils when you cut them out.

Turn to the last page of your flip book. Since you already know how to do this, and how to check if this paper works, we'll dive right in.

Start with the small fish. Begin tracing this stencil on this stack of pages so that the fish swims onto, across, and off the page. Once you have created this simple animation, try it out. Make sure that this little fish swims smoothly across the page.

Now it's time to add the large fish. Pick a frame that shows all of the smaller fish about halfway across the page. This is the frame where the large fish will enter. At the edge of this page, draw in a little bit of the large fish. Note that both fish should be separated by a small distance. As you draw each of the following frames, keep this distance the same for the entire chase.

Lower the next page. Here, the smaller fish should be slightly closer to swimming off the page. Draw in your second image of the large fish. Make sure that more of the large fish shows as you continue each frame.

Keep inserting, moving, and drawing the large fish until it has moved off the page.

Flip the pages and you'll see a slightly more complex animation.

What happens:

Flipping the pages creates an illusion of the large fish chasing the smaller fish.

Why:

By placing the traces of the large fish just after the smaller fish, you set the scene for a chase.

EYE TRICKS: HARDWIRED ILLUSIONS

Some illusions come from the way your visual system is put together. We'll call the optical tricks in this section the "hardwired" illusions. To best understand how they work, let's look at how the eye works.

All the sights you see begin with light energy, which travels through the air (or water or clear solids or empty space or whatever) and enters your eye. When light strikes the "screen" inside of the eye, it starts a chain of events that finishes up with an image in your mind of what you "see." Let's examine how the different parts of the eye do this.

The outer layers of your eye hold things together. Without this, the parts of your eye and the clear, jelly-like goo that fills the eyeball would spill out. In the front of the eye is a clear, protective covering called the *cornea*. It protects the eyes and helps focus light because the cornea is curved. People who wear contact lenses are familiar with this curve because it offers a surface to keep a contact lens from "swimming" all over the outside of the eyeball.

In the center of your eye is a tiny hole called the *pupil*. The pupil looks black because it has no color. It's just a hole for light to enter into the eye.

Surrounding the pupil is a muscle called the *iris*. The color of the iris is the color of your eye. It can be brown, green, hazel, or blue. Since the iris is a muscle, it can become larger and smaller. When the iris becomes smaller, the pupil opens wider and allows more light to come into the eye. When the iris becomes larger, the pupil closes and allows less light to come into the eye.

Light that enters the pupil goes through the *lens*. The lens is a clear muscle that focuses the light rays. It can wear down. That's why older people usually wear glasses or contact lenses. They make up for the lost use of the lens.

The back of the eyeball has a screen called the *retina*. It is sensitive to light. When light hits the retina, cells in the retina called *rods* and *cones* create nerve messages.

In the center of the retina is the *fovea*. The fovea has the greatest number of cones. When we see something, we try to look straight at it. That way, light falls on the fovea.

Messages made by the rods and cones follow a route to the brain. This route is called the *optic nerve*. When these messages reach the brain, they turn into the sights we see.

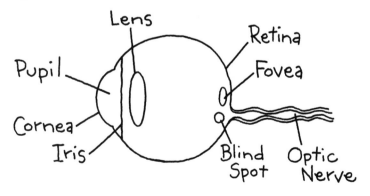

Blind Spot

You now know how the eye works to let you see what's in front of you. In this experiment, we'll find a way to *not* see what you're looking at.

You need:
marker
unruled paper

What to do:
Crease and tear out a thin strip (about 1 inch, 2.5 cm, wide) from a sheet of unruled paper. Use the marker to place a dot and an "X" on the strip as shown. Hold the strip so that the center of the strip touches the end of your nose. The "X" should be on the right side of your nose.

Close your right eye. Slowly move the strip away from your face. As you do, keep looking at the "X." At some point the dot will disappear. Hold the strip so that you can't see the dot with your left eye. Open your right eye. Can you see the dot using both eyes? Good. Remember that.

Close your right eye again. Continue moving the strip away. Does the dot disappear again?

Repeat this experiment using the other eye. Before you begin, remember to turn the strip around so that the "X" is on the left side of your nose. Close your left eye and move the strip away until you can't see the dot. Did this happen at the same distance as with the right eye?

What happens:
When the paper is at the correct distance, the dot disappears.

Why:
Light rays that pass into your eye are focused on the retina. As you have learned, the retina is sensitive to light. Cells in the retina create nerve signals that are sent to the brain through the optic nerve.

The optic nerve connects to the retina at a spot just below the fovea. There are no rods or cones here. Since this small area has nothing to notice the light, it is blind and, therefore, it is called a *blind spot*.

As you saw, even though the dot was lost in one eye's blind spot, the other eye noticed it. By the blind spots being in slightly different positions, one eye can fill in the information that is missed by the other eye's blind spot.

Where Have All the Colors Gone?

Colors need light—a good deal of it. Let's see why.

You need:
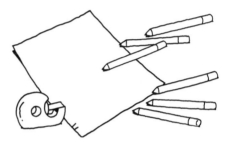
    six different-colored
       pencils
    unruled white paper
    tape

What to do:

Pick a colored pencil. What color is it? Good, you've done the difficult part. Using this pencil, write the name of the color on a sheet of white paper.

Select another pencil. Again, write the name of this color somewhere on the sheet of paper. Continue writing the names of the colors until you have used all of the pencils.

Tape the paper up on a nearby wall. In bright light, read the words. Notice how each word and the color in which it is written match?

Dim the lights in the room. Try reading the words again. Can you still make out the different colors? Which colors are easiest to read? Which colors are more difficult to make out?

What happens:

When the lights are low, it is difficult to make out colors.

Why:

Rods and cones pick up the light that enters your eyes. Rods are great at picking up low levels of light. In fact, they let us see at night or in dim rooms. But rods can't see colors. They view the world in shades of black and white.

Cones don't do very well in dim light. Cones need brighter light. But cones can see colors.

In bright light, your cones see the colors that you wrote with your pencil. When you dim the light, your cones don't have enough light to work. Instead, the words can only be seen by the rods and, therefore, appear as shades of gray.

Where Did You Get Those Shades?

Imagine a world in which you couldn't tell apart different colors. Reds, yellows, and blues would be seen as shades of gray—but would each color be seen as its own shade or would some colors have the same black-and-white appearance?

You need:

assortment of watercolor paints   mixing tray
paintbrush   paper

What to do:

Try painting the colors of a rainbow: red, orange, yellow, green, blue, and violet. Or create your own colors.

Dim the lights; stand back; pick two colors that now look alike. Here's your challenge: In low light, change one of these colors so its gray looks exactly like the other color.

What happens:

With careful mixing, you can make two different colors become the same shade of gray.

Why:

Again, it's because of the cones in your eyes not "seeing" well in dim light. When the light lowers, the cones don't work. Instead, the image is picked up by the rods, which can only see in shades of gray.

Field Trip

Everyone loves to go on a field trip. In this experiment, we'll be going on a field trip that explores visual fields. All you need is a nighttime sky that is clear and dark enough to see the stars. Let's go.

You need:

a clear and dark night

It's dark out!

What to do:

Wait until it's nighttime. Have an adult go with you to an open area outside. Look up into the sky.

Compare the brightness of the different stars and planets. Now pick a very faint star—the dimmest light in the sky.

Look directly at this dim star. Without shifting your gaze, see how its brightness compares with surrounding stars in your visual field. Remember that.

Now look slightly to the side of the dim star. What happens to its brightness? Is it easier or more difficult to see?

What happens:

It is easier to see a dim star when you don't look right at it. Instead, look slightly to its side.

Why:

Both rods and cones are not arranged evenly in the retina. There is a central spot at the back of the retina called the *fovea*. The fovea is full of cones. There are so many cones here that the fovea cannot see low light.

When you look directly at an object, its light is cast on the fovea. If the object is bright, the cones in the fovea pick up the light and create a rich, colorful image. If the light is dim, the cones will not respond.

To see dim objects, you should look slightly to the side of the object. This way, the light from the object doesn't fall on your fovea. Instead, it falls a little away from it onto an area that has lots of rods.

More Fieldwork

We're going back outside. This time, however, it will be during the day.

You need:

time to go outside

Avoid the sun!

What to do:

Go outside and look into the sky. Find an area of the sky that either has no clouds or is completely covered by clouds. *Do not look at the sun! Its powerful light rays can permanently damage and destroy parts of your eye!*

Keep looking up. Do you see any snakelike things floating in front of you? What happens when you try to look directly at them?

What happens:

Under the right lighting, you see tiny, long objects floating around your field of vision.

Why:

Your eyeball isn't empty. It's filled with a clear, jelly-like stuff. Without this jelly stuffing, the eyeball would fall in.

Although the jelly is clear, things can float in it. Often, these "floaters" are capillaries: tiny blood vessels that at one time helped bring food and oxygen to parts of your eye. When these capillaries break away from the eye tissue, they can wind up in this jelly. That's when you see them!

Pump Up the Difference

Suppose you placed a small piece of white paper on a larger sheet of the same paper. Most likely, you'd see the smaller piece. Although the difference in color between them may be very small, your eye is able to see the smaller piece by finding its "edge."

You need:

black construction paper
bright white background (tabletop or board)
scissors
ruler

What to do:

Use the ruler and scissors to cut out sixteen squares from the black construction paper. The sides of the squares should be about 2 inches (5.1 cm). Place the squares on a white table or board so that you have four rows of four squares. Keep the rows and columns evenly in line. Separate the squares by about the width of a pencil.

Look at the center of this huge square you've made. What do you see at the white center where the white lines crisscross? Look at the spot. What happens? Try moving the squares farther apart. At what distance does the illusion no longer work?

What happens:

Gray spots appear at the corners of the blocks. The spots disappear when you try to look straight at them.

Why:

The rods and cones in your eye "speak" to one another. How they speak to one another can either increase or reduce the light they see. Their goal is to help you notice the outlines of objects that you see.

When objects have the same shade, the rods and cones help separate the objects. For example, when you look at a white object in front of a white wall, you may not see much difference between the object and the wall. But the rods and cones increase the difference by making the object or wall look more gray.

In this experiment, the white center of where the blocks meet is surrounded by white on four sides. Your rods and cones go to work by making this center look darker than the lines connecting it. This creates an illusion of a dark spot at each crisscross.

This illusion happens because of the rods in your eyes. The rods, which are not in the center of your fovea, see things in black and white. When you look directly at the white center, its image falls mostly on the cones in your eyes. As a result, the spots seem to jump away!

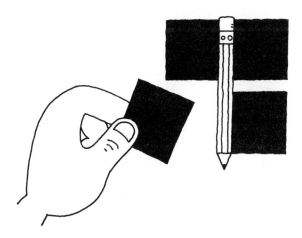

Not Fade Away

Suppose you left a pair of jeans lying out in the sun for several days. When you get them, you'll discover that the jeans faded in the sunlight. Here's why: Sunlight contains energy. When this energy strikes the fabric, it creates a chemical reaction that breaks down the color compounds in the jeans. As a result, the fabric becomes lighter in color.

You need:
black marker
sheet of white paper

What to do:
In the middle of the sheet of paper, use the marker to draw a small dot. Turn the paper over. Now use the marker to draw a large "X" in the middle of this side.

Stare at the center of the "X" for 10 seconds. Quickly turn the paper over. Stare at the dot. What do you see? How does this illusion compare with the original "X" target?

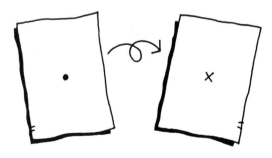

What happens:

A white "X" appears in the middle of the paper over where the dot is.

Why:

When you stare at the "X," the light rays fill your retina. There they break down a coloring agent in your eye called *visual purple*. With less visual purple, parts of the retina become less sensitive to light.

The parts of the retina where the dark "X" fell are protected from the light. The parts of the retina where light fell lose some visual purple.

After you stare at the "X" and then quickly look at the dot, your eyes don't have enough time to build back the lost visual purple. This area stays less sensitive to light. But the parts of the retina that didn't lose visual purple (the parts where the "X" fell) are still sensitive to light.

The side of the page with only the dot is mostly white. This white is "seen" by the entire retina. However, only the part of the retina with enough visual purple will respond. This produces a white "X" against a dark background.

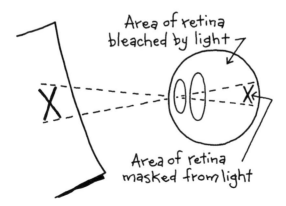

Area of retina bleached by light

Area of retina masked from light

Color Code

Smile! Your aunt shows off her new camera by taking an indoor picture of you. She is standing 2 inches (5.1 cm) away from you when the flash goes off. Do you see floating spots afterward?

You need:

red, green, blue, and yellow markers

What to do:

Look at the four rows of boxes on the opposite page. Each row has two boxes. The entire paint can in the box gets colored. The box with the "X" is where you will look to see the illusion.

Color the paint can in the top box red. Stay within the lines and fill in the entire can. Press down on the marker to make a rich, full color. Color the next paint can down blue. Then color the third paint can green. Finally, color the fourth paint can yellow.

Stare at the red paint can for 10 seconds. Then quickly look at the "X" in the uncolored box to the right of it. What do you see? Repeat this with the blue, green, and yellow paint cans. What color afterimage do you see after you look at each of the paint cans?

What happens:

The red paint can turns green when you stare at the "X" on the white page. The blue can turns yellow, the yellow can turns blue, and the green can turns red.

Why:

Afterimages are illusions that appear when your eyes look at the same thing for a long time, or when something like a camera flash goes off in front of you. Not all psychologists, scientists who study the mind, agree on how these colored afterimages work. Many think that these afterimages are produced by draining chemicals from the cones. Since the cones lose the ability to "see," they produce the wrong mix of color signals. Your brain sees this mix as a complementary color.

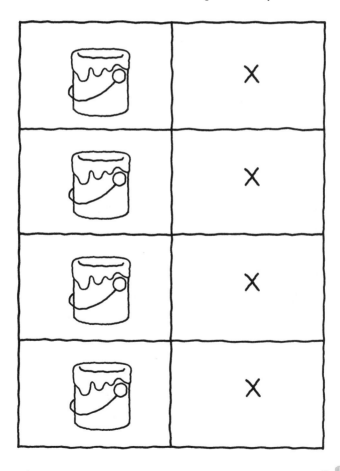

Pink Pigs

Now that you know about color afterimages, you can create some. We'll give you the pictures. You pick the color, but first, think about it. You'll need to pick a marker whose color creates the correct afterimage color.

You need:

unruled white paper   blank white wall
pink, green, blue, and yellow markers

What to do:

Look at the pictures and the names below them. Choose a color that will give each picture the right afterimage color. For example, if the name says "pink flamingo,"

pink pig

yellow flower

blueberries

green caterpillar

you'll need to fill the correct color so that its afterimage will be in pink.

Trace and color in these four objects on white paper: 1. pink pig; 2. green caterpillar; 3. blueberries (don't forget the green stems); 4. yellow flower (don't forget the green stems here as well).

Once you've colored in all the images, stare at the pig for about 10 seconds. Then look at a white wall. What appears? Does the afterimage have the correct color? Do this for each of the objects.

What happens:
Images of pink pigs, green caterpillars, blueberries, and yellow flowers appear on the wall.

Why:
As you stare at each of the colored objects, you fill your eyes with its color. This causes a shift in the chemistry of your eye. If you picked the right colors, you'll have made the correct shift to give you the right afterimage color.

What are the colors you need to use? Sorry, we're not telling. If you didn't get them the first time, keep trying and then move on to the next four objects below.

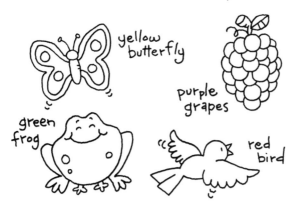

yellow butterfly

purple grapes

green frog

red bird

Balancing Act

Fluorescent light, such as the light in your kitchen, makes a strong, green-blue shade that colors all of the objects brightened in this light. But when you stand beneath these lights, things look pretty normal. How come?

Your visual system balances your world. It continually "corrects" the colors you see so that everything stays normal. Want to see what happens when we trick this color correction?

You need:
different colored see-through plastic (from report covers, lighting gels, or packaging cellophane)
white wall

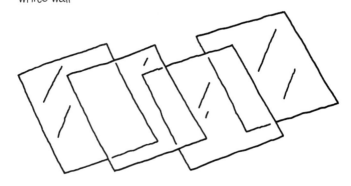

What to do:
Hold one of the colored plastics over one eye. Place it at the tip of your nose, keeping it away from touching your eye.

Keep the plastic in place for several minutes. As you look around the room, see the difference between what each eye sees. Do you get used to the color of the plastic? How can you tell?

Remove the plastic and look at a white wall. Close each eye and compare the view you see through each eye. Do the colors now look the same? What happens to the view that you saw looking through the colored plastic?

What happens:
When the colored plastic is removed, the eye creates an image that is lightly colored.

Why:
The "tinting," or light coloring, happens after the color is corrected. When the cones in your eye become filled with one color, they lose their sensitivity to this color. The result is an increase in noticing its complementary color. Suppose you are looking through a piece of green plastic. Your brain will try to balance out the green by adding a red tint. When the green filter is removed, your brain will take a moment to change. For several seconds it will add unneeded color and make your world appear pink.

A Different Spin on Color Perception

Did you know that white isn't what it appears? Unlike red, orange, yellow, green, blue, and violet, white isn't a true color. Instead, white is what our brains create when our eyes pick up the combination of different colors.

You need:

red, blue, and green markers
bead of modeling clay
pushpin
small DC motor with wire leads (from battery-operated toy)

heavy-stock white paper
1.5 volt AA battery
scissors

What to do:

Photocopy, trace, or cut out and paste this disk onto a sheet of heavy-stock white paper. Use your scissors to carefully cut out this disk.

Use your markers to color in the slices of the disk with the indicated color. You'll get the best results by using deep and dark colors.

Use a pushpin to punch a hole in the center of the pattern.

Place a bead-sized lump of clay on the tip end of the motor's shaft. This clay will stick the disk to the shaft. Insert the shaft with the clay

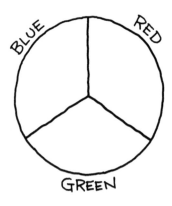

into the disk hole. Make sure that the clay holds to both the paper and the metal shaft so that the disk doesn't slip.

Place the two leads of the motor to the opposite ends of an AA battery.

Look at the colors. What happens to them as the disk spins? When do they appear separate? When do they combine?

You can play with the final color by changing the size of the color slices. If your final color is too green, make a new disk using a smaller "slice" of green. If there's too little red, increase the red area. It's all up to you!

What happens:

The spinning colors come together to create a white or light gray mix.

Why:

No one is certain what causes this. Some psychologists believe that the red, blue, and green stay in your brain long enough so that they combine to create white. Other psychologists believe that this happens because the cones become confused when they "speak" to one another.

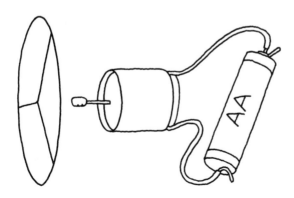

Colors in Black and White

In 1838, a scientist named G. T. Fechner discovered that a spinning pattern of black and white could create imaginary colors. These effects are called "Fechner lines." Fechner lines can be seen in all sort of spinning patterns, including the one we'll make here.

You need:

black marker
pushpin
paste
scissors
bead of modeling clay
heavy-stock white paper
small DC motor with wire leads
 (from battery-operated toy)

What to do:

Photocopy, trace, or cut out and paste this pattern onto a sheet of heavy-stock paper. Use your scissors to carefully cut out this disk.

Carefully punch a hole in the center of the pattern using a pushpin.

Place a bead-sized lump of clay on the tip end of the motor's shaft. Insert the clay into the disk hole. Make sure that the clay fills the gap between the paper and the metal shaft so that the disk doesn't slip.

Place the two leads of the motor to the opposite ends of an AA battery.

Look at the spinning pattern. What happens? Try touching and removing the leads to slow down the spin of the disk. Does a different speed affect the illusion?

What happens:

The spinning pattern creates imaginary colors called *Fechner lines*.

Why:

No one knows for certain. Some scientists think it has to do with how fast a cone can send signals. When a black-and-white image changes too quickly, some cones can't react quickly enough. This produces a mixed-up message that your brain thinks is a color.

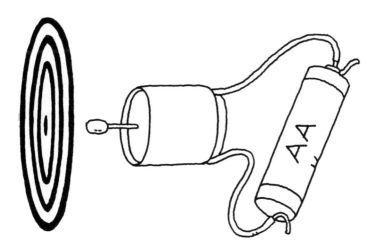

STRETCHING THE TRUTH: DISTORTIONS OF LENGTH AND SIZE

Did you know that your brain has written a reference book? The pages of this book are made from experiences of things you've seen. Light that is picked up by your eyes is changed into nerve signals. These signals are sent out along the optic nerve to the brain. Within the brain, the signals are gathered and decoded. This information is compared to things you have seen before.

When something appears the same, your brain applies what it already knows about this subject to the new image. This helps your brain make sense of what you are seeing. For example, when you enter a new room, your brain automatically changes shapes and sizes to fit what a room normally looks like. From your old experiences, you quickly made a visual scene that makes the most sense.

Optical illusions—especially those that trick us into changing length, size, and shape—most often come from applying the wrong rules. Our brain gets fooled by misleading signals and incorrectly makes out what our eyes see. When the wrong rules are applied, your brain creates a distorted view called an *optical illusion*.

Illusionary Lengths

Here's an illusion you may have seen. Look at the two standing lines below. How do they compare? To most people, AB appears slightly longer than CD.

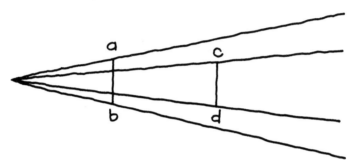

Using a ruler, measure both lines. Surprised? Although they don't look it, AB and CD are the exact same length.

Now let's experiment with this effect on everyday objects such as paper clips, coins, and toothpicks.

You need:

ruler	pencil
two paper clips, coins,	marker
and same-size toothpicks	sheet of unruled paper

What to do:

Place your sheet of paper on top of a table. Turn the page so that the longer length is sideways. (This is called *landscape* orientation.) Use your ruler and pencil to lightly draw a line across the middle of the paper, dividing it into an upper and lower half. Place a dot on this line about 1 inch (2.5 cm) from the left side of the paper. Lightly draw a line going up and down through this point. Your page should look like this:

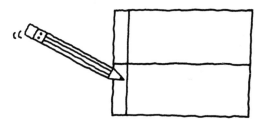

Use your marker to draw a line from the two lines' meeting point to the top right corner of the page. Draw a second line from the point to the bottom right corner of the page.

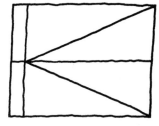

Make two more marks on the right edge of the paper. The marks should be placed halfway between each corner to the middle line. Use your marker to draw two more dark lines connecting each mark with the point where the lines meet.

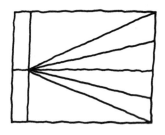

Place one paper clip on this drawing so that its ends touch the highest and the lowest lines. Place the other paper clip farther along the pattern so that the ends of this clip touch the top and the bottom lines of the smaller angle.

When it is finished, it should look something like this:

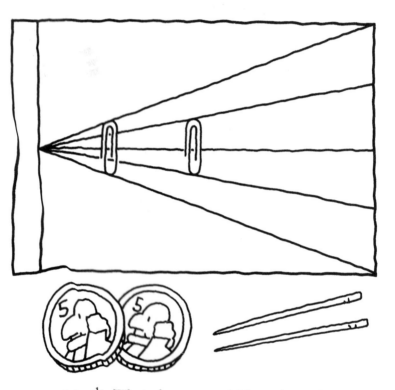

Stand back. What do you see? How does changing the positions of the paper clips affect the illusion? Are some positions better than others for creating this illusion? Try using the toothpicks to compare.

Now let's use two coins that are the same size. Does the illusion still work with round objects?

Try adding two more lines to form a third angle. When this third angle is complete, see what happens when you use three objects of the same size. Does the illusion still work? Do all three objects appear different in size?

What happens:

The paper clip, coin, or toothpick closest to where all the lines meet appears larger than the object that is farther away.

Why:

Scientists don't agree on why this happens. Some think the brain automatically "shrinks" objects that are in open spaces. The paper clip closest to where the lines meet has a bunch of lines behind it; the clip farthest away has no lines behind it. Your brain picks this up and shrinks the clip that has no lines behind it.

Other scientists think that the way the angles are arranged makes it look three-dimensional. In other words, your brain thinks that some of the lines are closer to you while other lines are farther away. That's when the "trouble" begins.

When the paper clips are placed over the lines, your brain falls back to its wrong idea about depth. It "stretches" the paper clip that is closest to where the lines come together. At the same time, it "shrinks" the paper clip that is farther away. What happens is an incorrect comparison known as a *distortion of length*.

Would changing how wide apart or close together the lines are affect the illusion? Would making the lines farther apart make the illusion stronger? Or would they "wash out" this confusing effect? Try it and find out!

Room for Mistakes

In the last experiment, you saw that simple angles can create a false sense of depth. This leads to an illusion of length. But what happens when you arrange angles to create something that looks like a room or hallway? How might the look of a "real scene" affect the illusion? Will the illusion be stronger or weaker? Let's find out.

You'll use this line drawing to see how a "real scene" creates illusions. Don't be limited by these pages. You can use this drawing as a model for creating your own bigger pattern.

You need:
several coins, charms,
or postage stamps of the same size

What to do:
Place two coins anywhere on the pattern. Stand back. Do the objects still appear the same size, or does one look bigger than the other?

Add another coin. See how putting the different coins at different places affects their size.

What happens:
The objects that are placed at the lower left-hand corner of the hallway look smaller than the same objects placed in the upper right-hand corner.

Why:

Your brain loves to use its book of rules. When you see this image, your brain thinks that this drawing is three-dimensional. The back walls look far away and small. As a result, all the same-size objects, depending on where you put them on the drawing, look larger or smaller.

Tracks of the Trade

Railroad tracks make a great pattern for creating illusions of length. Like angles and hallways, an image of railroad tracks disappearing in the distance gives you a sense of a three-dimensional scene.

You need:
copy of a train or model railroad magazine
scissors

What to do:
Search through the pages of train magazines for a picture that shows a set of railroad tracks. A local hobby store would be the best place to find such a magazine. The best picture for our illusion would show the tracks coming straight at you, like our drawing on the next page, and be about the size of an entire page.

Use your scissors to cut out these two trains.

Place one of the trains at the front of
the tracks. Put the other train farther
back on the tracks.

Compare the size of the trains.
Do they appear the same size? If
not, which one looks larger?

Now try using paper clips,
checkers, or coins on the
tracks. Does the illusion
still work?

What happens:

The object at the top of the tracks looks larger than the
same-size object at the bottom of the tracks.

Why:

The train tracks create a three-dimensional scene. It is so
strong that it tricks your brain into thinking that this
picture is not flat. When the trains are placed on the
track, your brain uses its old experiences of seeing train
tracks to change what it sees. In doing so, it creates a
distortion of size and gives depth to this flat image .

Your brain first sees these two trains to be the same
size, but since it believes that the train tracks are three-
dimensional, it changes the information it receives. The
brain believes that if the trains are the same size in the
picture, the one that seems farther away must be larger.
This makes sense because in order for a faraway object
to appear as large as a closer one, the faraway one
must be bigger. This idea tricks your brain into looking
at the picture again and increasing the size of the train
that appears farther away.

Adding Arrowheads

The two lines below are the same length. But by adding a few extra lines, you'll create another illusion of length.

You need:
marker

What to do:
Draw an arrowhead to each end of the top line; they should point outward. Now draw an arrowhead to each end of the bottom line; they should point inward.

Stand back and look at the lines. Do they still look the same length?

What happens:
You have just made the Müller-Lyer illusion, which was created in 1889; students still have it on their notebooks and book covers. As you see, when the arrows point inward, the line seems longer.

Why:
Scientists still aren't certain why this happens. Some think we are tricked into thinking we see in three dimensions, "seeing" the top line closer than the bottom line. Then, our 3-D thinking automatically shrinks the line we think is closer. At the same time, our 3-D thinking stretches the line we think is farther away, creating the illusion of different lengths.

Rulers Don't Lie . . . Right?

Here's your chance to bend some rules with rulers. As you can see, we've given you a set of rulers to play with. Your challenge is to create the Müller-Lyer illusion (done in the last experiment) using these rulers.

You need:

marker   ruler

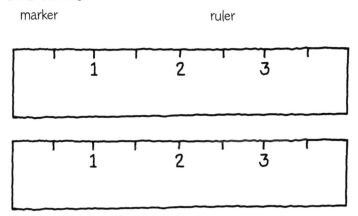

What to do:

Use the top ruler. Draw a thick line along the edge of the ruler from the 0-inch to the 1-inch mark. At each end of this line, add an arrowhead that points outward. Draw a second line from the 2-inch to the 3-inch mark. At each end of this line, add an arrowhead that points inward. How do these two lines compare? Which one looks longer? Is it?

Let's use the bottom ruler. Draw a thick line along the ruler from the 0-inch to the 2-inch mark. Add an arrowhead that points outward at the end of the 0-inch mark. Add an arrowhead that points inward at the end of the 2-inch mark. Now add another arrowhead that points to the right of the 1-inch mark. How do the lines made from the bottom ruler compare? Does the illusion still work when the two parts of this line are joined?

What happens:
Even though the lines of each ruler are the same, they still look to be different lengths.

Why:
It's the Müller-Lyer illusion at work again. It happens in both the connected and separated lines.

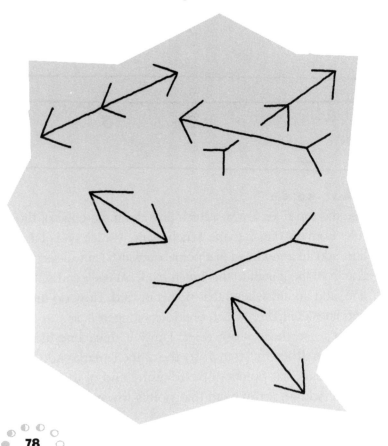

Coining an Illusion

So far, the illusions you've made changed the appearance of lines. Some lines looked longer. Others looked shorter.

In this experiment, you'll find out if you really need lines. In other words, can you use the same illusion effect on empty space? Can space be stretched? Can it be shrunk? There's one way to find out: experiment.

You need:

twelve coins that are the
  same size
ruler

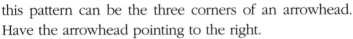

What to do:

Arrange three coins into a triangle. As you can see, this pattern can be the three corners of an arrowhead. Have the arrowhead pointing to the right.

Using your ruler, measure 6 inches (15.3 cm) from the tip of this arrowhead. At the end of the 6 inches (15.3 cm), arrange three coins to make another arrowhead, pointing to the left. Make sure that the tip of this arrowhead is at the 6-inch (15.3 cm) mark.

Using your ruler, measure another 6 inches (15.3 cm) and line it up evenly below the two arrowheads.

Using three coins for each arrowhead, make two more arrowheads. This time, make the arrowheads point outward.

Does the illusion still work?

What happens:

The space between the arrowheads that point inward looks greater than the space between the arrowheads that point outward.

Why:

Once again, it's the old Müller-Lyer effect working. This time it shrinks and stretches empty space.

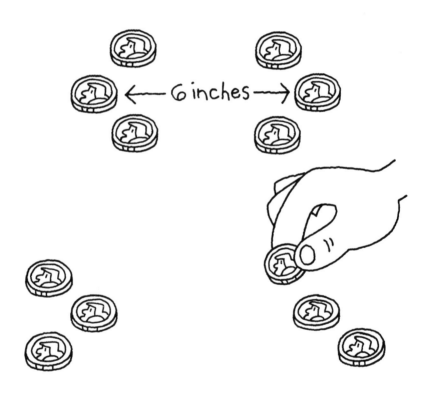

More Coinage

Hold on to those coins from our last experiment. You'll need them. In fact, you'll have to get a bunch of different coins for this next visual trick.

You need:
    two medium-sized coins
    five small coins
    five large coins

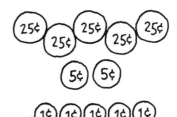

What to do:

Place the two medium-sized coins on the floor. They should be about a hand's distance apart.

Put the five large coins around one of the medium coins. These large coins should touch the medium coin and be the same distance from one another. When you're

done, the large coins will make the five points of a regular pentagon (a five-sided figure).

Put the five small coins around the other medium-sized coin. Place them in the same pattern as the large coins.

Stand up. Look down at the two medium-sized coins. Do they appear to be the same size, or is one slightly larger than the other?

What happens:

The coin surrounded by the large coins looks smaller than the coin surrounded by the small coins.

Why:

Your brain is constantly comparing images to what's around them. It measures the size of one thing against another. One medium-sized coin looks small because it is surrounded by larger objects. Likewise, the medium-sized coin that is surrounded by small coins seems to be a bit larger than it is.

Tricky Trapezoids

Can the way you arrange two shapes create an optical illusion? Let's find out.

You need:
scissors
construction paper
ruler

What to do:
Copy this figure onto a scrap of construction paper. This figure is called a trapezoid.

Use your scissors to cut out the pattern. Trace this pattern that you've cut out onto another piece of construction paper. Cut out this second pattern. Presto! You now have two of the same trapezoid.

Place the trapezoids so that the longer bottoms face each other like this:

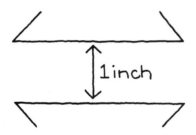

Keep the edges apart by about 1 inch (2.5 cm). Compare the sizes of the two trapezoids. Do they appear to be the same size? Does one look larger than the other?

Now place the two trapezoids so that their shorter tops face each other.

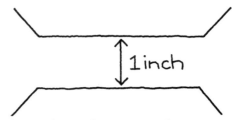

Remember to keep the trapezoids separated. Do they still look the same size?

Turn only one of the trapezoids so that its longer bottom faces the shorter top of the other figure. What happens to their appearance? Does one look larger than the other?

What happens:

When the longer bottoms face each other, both trapezoids appear to be the same size. Likewise, when the shorter tops face each other, the trapezoids appear equal in size. But when the shorter top faces the longer base, the trapezoid with the longer bottom appears larger.

Why:

When the longer side of an object is placed evenly against the shorter side of an object, your brain automatically thinks that the longer side comes from a bigger object. It makes sense. From experience, that's often the way things have been. Your brain sticks to the shortcut. So even though these trapezoids are the same size, the one that presents its longer side looks bigger than the one with the shorter side.

TILTS, TWISTS, AND TOPSY-TURVIES:
JUMBLE OF BUMBLE

Scientists don't know everything. In fact, after studying optical illusions for over one hundred years, they still can't agree on how some of them work. Maybe *you* will be the one who can give the perfect explanation so that everyone will finally agree.

This section offers all kinds of optical illusions that still confuse scientists. It also offers a great place for thinking. Can you try to find the explanations for these illusions based upon what you've already seen? How will your explanations compare with the best guesses of scientists?

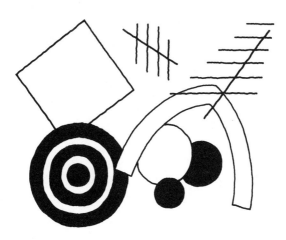

A New Slant on Things

Look at the set of slanted lines below. They are *parallel,* which means they don't come together or spread apart. The magic we're going to make will change the look of these lines.

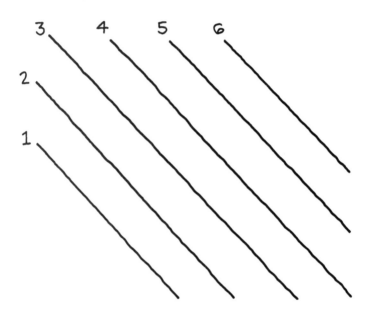

You need:
marker
ruler

What to do:
To create this illusion, add a set of lines crossing each of the slanted lines. Use a ruler to help create straight lines and keep the lines the same distance apart.

Add horizontal lines, lines that run across, to the odd-numbered lines. Make vertical lines, lines that stand, to the even-numbered lines.

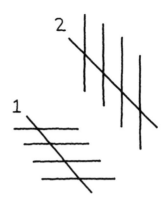

Here's a small part of what it should look like:

Draw the lines short so they don't touch any of the other lines. Once you're done, look at the slanted lines. Do they still look parallel?

What happens:

The lines you drew make you "see" the parallel lines spread apart or come together at opposite ends.

Why:

Even though this illusion has been studied since the 1860s, psychologists can't all agree on why we see its effect. Some think it has to do with giving the brain too much information. The repeating lines are too much for the brain to gather. Others think we use the angle of the cross lines to set the slant of the parallel lines.

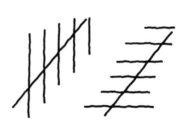

What do you think?

Bending In

For this illusion, we'll offer a confusing background. You supply the straight sides of the figure.

You need:
marker
ruler

What to do:
Make a square connecting the dots at A, B, C, and D. Use a ruler when you draw your lines. This way, they'll be straight.

Does your perfect square appear perfect?

What happens:
The sides of the square seem to bend inward.

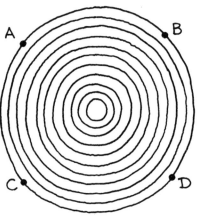

Why:
No one knows for certain, but psychologists do agree that a pattern of circles within circles (known as *concentric* circles) makes a background that can easily bend shapes that are drawn over it.

Warp Speed

This time we've drawn a square. Your assignment is to add a confusing background pattern.

You need:
marker
ruler

What to do:
Use your ruler to draw ten straight lines. These lines should all begin at the mark above the square and connect to each of the dots below the square.

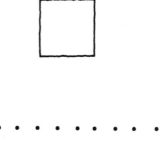

After drawing the pattern, look at the square again. Does the appearance of the square change?

What happens:
The sides of the square appear slightly slanted.

Why:
One explanation says that the lines create a three-dimensional look to this drawing. Your brain adds depth to what your eyes see so that the square appears slightly slanted.

Upside Downside

Look into a mirror and what do you see? A world where the right and left are reversed. Some things, like words, may be hard to make out. But for the most part, it is not too confusing.

But imagine a world that is upside down. Now that becomes a *very* different place. It is too much for your brain to make sense out of a topsy-turvy world. This can lead to all sorts of confusion and optical illusions.

You need:

photograph of a face from a magazine
scissors
heavy-stock paper

ruler
glue stick

What to do:

Find a page in a magazine that has a photograph of someone looking straight at you. Make sure nobody needs this magazine before you carefully tear this page out.

Use a ruler to draw rectangles around both eyes and the mouth. Make sure that you center the eyes and mouth within the drawn rectangles.

Use your scissors to carefully cut out each rectangle. Use your glue stick to paste the page (without its rectangles) onto a sheet of heavy stock paper.

Use your glue stick to paste the rectangle pieces back into their right spaces, but paste them *upside down*.

Turn the page upside down. Challenge a friend to find anything strange about this picture. Do the eyes or mouth give its upside-down change away?

Turn the page so that the model's face is right-side up. How does the person look now?

What happens:

When the head is upside down, you aren't aware that the eyes and mouth were spun around.

Why:

It is too much for your brain to make sense of the upside-down face. As a result, it doesn't pay attention to "small" things like the eyes and mouth being flipped over. To be fair to your brain, why should it even think that the eyes are flipped over? You've probably never seen someone who looks like this, so the experience doesn't appear in your brain's rule book.

Arch Enemy

Although you probably don't consider fettuccine a very strong material, it can easily break up the appearance of an arch.

You need:

a piece of uncooked fettuccine

What to do:

Examine the arch shown below. No tricks. It appears to be your usual arch.

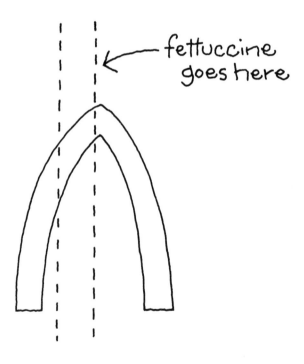

fettuccine goes here

Place a piece of uncooked fettuccine inside the dotted lines so that it cuts the arch into two unequal sections. The fettuccine can be any length, just as long as it covers the length shown on the dotted lines.

Stand back. Does the fettuccine cause any change in the appearance of the arch?

What happens:
The two sections do not appear to belong to the same arch.

Why:
The fettuccine interrupts the curve of the arch. Instead of following the smooth curve, you look down to follow the edge of the fettuccine. This "drop" in attention is enough to suggest that the curve also "drops," and therefore the arch doesn't appear to be connected.

Ruler Interference

Most of the time, a ruler is a helpful tool that can help you see things more accurately. But sometimes a ruler can just get in the way.

You need:
wooden or colored
  plastic ruler

What to do:

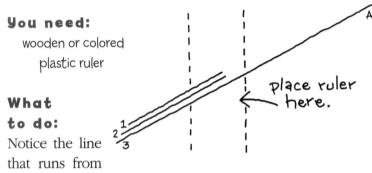

Notice the line that runs from Point A to Point 3. Now place the ruler between the dotted lines. It doesn't matter how much of the lines is hidden by the ruler as long as the ends of Lines 1, 2, and 3 are covered. Does Point A still appear to be on the same line as Point 3?

What happens:
The line from Point A looks like it is connected to either line of Point 1 or 2.

Why:
As in the last experiment, this ruler creates a slight change in your attention. This causes you to mistake how the partially hidden line continues.

Setting a Side Aside

An image that goes back and forth between two logical appearances is called an unstable figure. In the unstable figures below, you can see a cube popping out on the right or the left side. Which side did you see it on first?

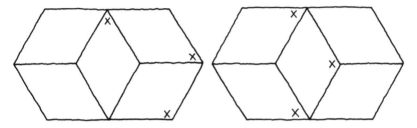

You need:
crayon or marker

What to do:
In each of the figures above, color in the three areas that have the "X." Does filling in these areas change the way you see the unstable figures?

What happens:
The colors help identify the parts of this figure that can represent a cube.

Why:
The same colors suggest that these sections are closely related and most likely part of the same figure. Your brain uses this suggestion to look at this figure as a colored cube and a background pattern.

Comparing Colors

Did you know that the way you view a color can change? How your brain picks up a shade of color depends on the other colors around it. Want to see it?

You need:
different colored markers

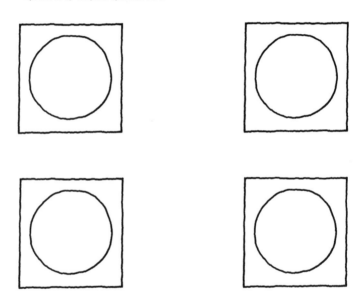

What to do:
Use the same color marker to fill in both top circles. Then use a different color marker to fill in the area between one filled-in circle and its surrounding square. Use the third marker to fill in the surrounding area of the second circle.

You decide on what colors you'd like to use. For the strongest effects, try using a light to medium shade for the circle. Make sure that you press evenly with the marker when you are coloring in the circle.

How do the circle colors compare? Try other colors in the bottom set of figures.

What happens:

The circle surrounded by the darker color appears slightly lighter than the same-colored circle surrounded by a lighter color.

Why:

Compare, compare, compare. Your brain bases the color of the circle on how the shades compare to their surroundings. Some psychologists believe that this effect is caused by increasing the difference between the color of the circle and the color that is around it. Other psychologists think that your brain wrongly makes the circles light or dark because of the way they appear against different backgrounds.

Imaginary Square

Put one thing on top of another and what happens? From experience, you've learned that the object on top blocks out your view of whatever is on the bottom. From what isn't covered, you can figure out the shape of the top object.

You need:
- scissors
- pencil
- ruler
- black construction paper
- sheet of white paper

What to do:
Use your ruler and pencil to copy this shape onto a sheet of black construction paper. Use your scissors to cut out this shape. Now trace it three times on the same construction paper to make three more copies. When you are finished, you'll have four of these shapes.

Place the four pieces on a sheet of white paper. Put each of the shapes at the corner of an imaginary square. Make sure the corners face inward and line up along the imaginary sides of this square. Although this square can be any size, place the corners so that the length of the sides are about 4 inches (10.2 cm).

Stand back. Can you see the square? How does the brightness of this "square" compare with the brightness of the background?

What happens:

You see an imaginary square whose four corners are made by the four pieces.

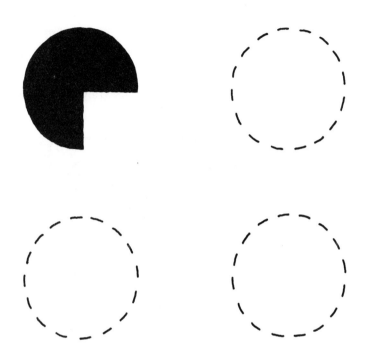

Why:

Your brain gets confused when it sees shapes that it isn't familiar with. It tries to make sense of this scene by looking at it in terms of *overlap*, or one thing being on top of another. The simplest and most familiar image is a white "square" that overlaps each of the four black circles. Your brain accepts this image and makes an imaginary square. Naturally, since the square is on top of the background, it should look slightly brighter. Your brain does the rest and creates this imaginary square that is lighter than its background.

Mosaic Madness

Take a look at the image below. Sure, it's blocky, but it contains a famous person—a guy with a beard. Do you see him yet? Squint your eyes, or take a few steps back and then look at this page. You can also find this guy on a penny.

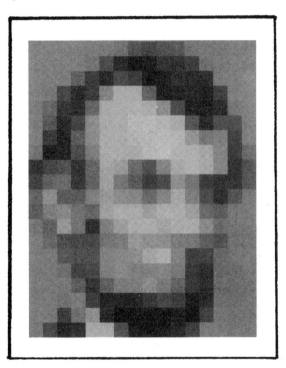

You need:

tracing paper

pencil

ruler

tape

different colored pencils

magazine

What to do:

Use a ruler and pencil to draw a grid on a sheet of tracing paper. The square boxes of this grid should be about 3/8 inch (1 cm) on each side.

From a magazine that no one needs anymore, find a full-page picture of a head. Tape the tracing paper over it. Notice how each box has a mix of colors.

Examine each box and decide on the "average" color for that box. Choose that color from your group of pencils. Use it to completely fill in the box. Continue filling in the boxes in this way until the whole photo has been copied in this style.

Take the tracing paper off the magazine page and tape it against a white wall.

How does it look up close? From across the room? What happens at a great enough distance?

What happens:

When you look at the tracing paper from a distance, the checkered pattern becomes a smooth photograph.

Why:

When you are looking at the tracing paper up close, your eyes can see each of the blocks that form the checkered pattern, or mosaic. Therefore, they look at this mosaic as a bunch of separate blocks. In a way, this is like seeing only the trees and not the forest.

At a distance, your eyes can no longer spot each of the blocks. They are too far away. Instead, all of the blocks blend together and create the illusion of a "whole" image. Since you can't make out each block, it's like seeing the forest and not the trees.

FANTASTIC FLAT-SCREEN PHANTOMS:
ILLUSIONS OF DEPTH

Your retina is a screen found in the back of your eyeball. Although your retina is curved, its surface is flat. So any image that appears on your retina is two-dimensional. Yet you see your world in three dimensions. Why?

Overlap, which is when one object blocks another, helps you see in 3-D. When things are blocked, your brain immediately creates a scene that sets up the distance between the objects. It uses logic and experience to place the object that appears unchanged closer to you and the object that is blocked farther away.

Another clue to 3-D is the object's speed. Objects that are closer to you appear to move quicker than objects that are farther away. You can check this out by waving your hand in front of your face. When your hand is farther away, it takes longer to move it across your face.

Brightness offers another clue to an object's distance. Closer items usually appear brighter than farther ones.

The strongest way to tell depth is from your binocular vision. "Binocular" refers to two eyes. Your two eyes help set things apart. The distance between your eyes puts what you see at slightly different views. By studying the difference between these views, your brain can figure out the distance between objects.

Dominant View

Before exploring our selection of three-dimensional illusions, let's do an experiment on binocular vision.

You need:
one finger

What to do:
Hold up a finger. Shut one eye and look at the finger. Now open both eyes. Did the finger jump when you viewed it with two eyes? Repeat this experiment, but use the other eye first. Did the finger jump this time?

What happens:
Your finger "jumps" only when you first look at it with your weaker eye.

Why:
You have a dominant, or stronger, eye. Your brain relies more on this eye to put together most of its sense of depth and placement of objects. When you view your finger only with your dominant eye, the position of your finger is set on the background. When you open your other eye, the position of your finger and its background stay the same. If you first looked at your finger with your recessive, or weaker, eye, its position will change when you open your dominant eye. Your finger will "jump" to adjust to what your dominant eye sees.

Come Together

Your brain can normally deal with slightly different images coming in from each eye. It applies a little bit of adjusting and overlaps the images. How easily they overlap helps your brain decide on the distance. But suppose you were given too much information for your brain? You be the judge.

You need:

marker
paper

 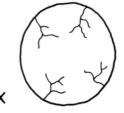

X

What to do:

Slowly bring your nose to the page toward the "X." What happens to the two images at the sides of the "X"?

Using this same idea, create your own pair of images. You can try drawing an arrow and bull's-eye, or a fish and fishbowl.

Keep each image the same distance from the "X" as shown in the above drawing. Use heavy lines to draw them so that the images won't fade. Have fun!

What happens:

The images appear to come together.

Why:

When you bring the paper close enough to you, your brain finds it easier to overlap these images than to keep them apart. When they come together, your brain accepts the logical scene.

Handy Hole-in-One

Here's another mind trick that will challenge how you see your world.

You need:
sheet of paper

Protect your eyes!

What to do:
Roll a sheet of paper into a tube.

CAUTION: To protect yourself from poking your eye, wrap the index finger and thumb of your right hand around the end of the tube that you are looking through. Your fingers will protect your eye.

Carefully bring the tube to your right eye. Place your left hand midway down the length of the tube. Make sure your left hand is opened with palm facing you.

Look ahead with both eyes open. Your right eye should be looking out through the tube. Your left eye should be looking at your left palm.

What do you see? Do the images remain separate?

What happens:
It appears as if you have a hole in your hand.

Why:

Different messages are sent to the brain. Your right eye sends to your brain what it sees through the tube. Your left eye sees only your left hand.

Since your brain has learned to bring the right- and left-eye images together, it forms a mix of these two views. It is tricked into creating an image in which a hole is placed in the center of your palm.

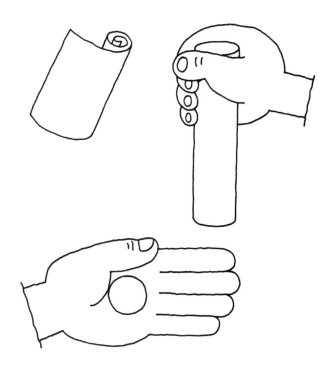

Stereo Pairs

Now we'll explore all sorts of three-dimensional illusions. We'll begin with some basic illusions. Once you know how to do them, we'll give you more difficult examples.

You need:

two sheets of paper

Protect your eyes!

What to do:

Roll each sheet into a tube. Remember, to prevent yourself from poking your eyes, wrap your index finger and thumb around the end of the tube that you will be looking through before bringing it to your eye. In this experiment, you'll need to do it with both hands because you are now looking through two tubes.

Notice that you have three pairs of images to examine on the opposite page. Each pair has a left-eye and right-eye image. Use your rolled tubes to look at these pairs.

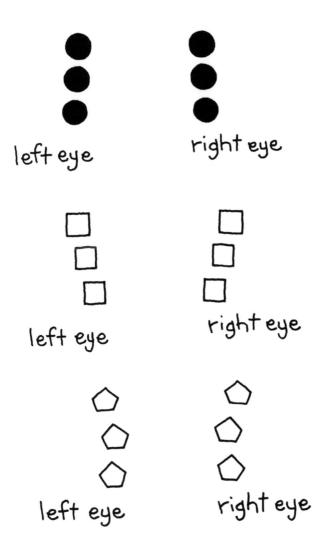

left eye

right eye

left eye

right eye

left eye

right eye

Place the bottom end of each tube about a finger's thickness above the page. This will offer enough space for light to fall on the images.

Look down the tubes. At first you may see two separate images. Keep looking. Within a few moments, the images will begin to move together. When this begins to happen, relax. Don't fight it. Let the right and left views come together into a single image.

Look at the image. Does it have depth? If it does, do all the parts of the image rise up to the same height? Do some parts of the image appear higher than others? If so, which ones?

Can you see how the distance between the right and left images compare to the height to which each image rises?

What happens:

When the right and left images come together, they create a three-dimensional image. In the group of circles, the top pair of circles rises higher than the other pairs of circles. In the group of squares, the bottom pair of squares rises higher. But in the last group, unlike the other groups, it is the middle pentagons that rise the highest.

Why:

When your brain overlaps the images, it uses how far apart the images are to determine depth. The squares, circles, and pentagons that are farthest apart are the most difficult to overlap. Your brain makes these objects appear lowest. Those that are closest together are easier to overlap and so they appear to rise highest off the paper.

Free Viewing

By now you should be able to bring right and left images together when you look through viewing tubes. If not, go back and practice with the tubes until you can. Once you can do it, you're ready to do this next experiment.

You need:
two sheets of paper (if necessary)

What to do:
Now that you know how to look through viewing tubes, we're going to take them away.

Look directly above these two images. Find a comfortable viewing height. Relax and let the views drift into a single image. Keep trying until you can do it.

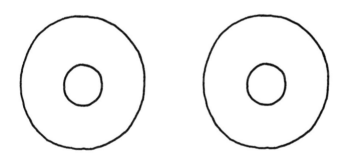

If the images won't come together after a few minutes, you can use the viewing tubes from the last experiment. Place one tube over each image. Lift the ends of the tubes off the paper so that some light can fall on them. Wrap your fingers around the ends of the tubes that you'll be looking through. Relax and keep looking. The circles will drift together.

Once you've seen the images come together with the tubes, try it again without the tubes. Relax. Let the images drift together. If you need to, use the viewing tubes again until you learn how to look at the images without the tubes.

This may take some practice, so don't give up. After a while you will be able to bring these images together without using your viewing tubes.

What happens:

The right and left images drift together into a single image. The inner circle appears to float above the larger outer circle.

Why:

It's the same science as in the last experiment. This time, however, you don't need the help of the viewing tubes. Being able to bring the images together without them is called *free viewing*.

Two-Level Float

By creating the same distance that separates images, you can create rows that appear to float at different levels. Here's a simple two-level float.

You need:

ability to free-view

What to do:

Relax and free-view this image.

BACK   BACK   BACK
FRONT FRONT FRONT

Use the viewing tubes if you can't bring the images together without them. But after you use the tubes, put them away and try to do this on your own. Practice making the image three-dimensional without using the tubes.

What happens:

The "front" appears to float slightly above the "back."

Why:

The words that form the "front" pattern are closer together than the words that form the "back" pattern. Therefore, when you overlap these words, the "front" appears to come closer to you.

Wallpaper

Using your brain to overlap patterns to make three-dimensional images isn't a new discovery. This optical trick, called the wallpaper effect, has been around since the 1800s.

You need:
twelve coins of the same size

What to do:
Place the coins into three rows with each row containing four coins. Separate each of the coins in the bottom row by 1/2 inch (1.2 cm). Keep all of the distances equal.

Separate each of the coins in the middle row by about 5/8 inch (1.6 cm). Again, keep this distance equal across the row.

Finally, separate each of the coins in the top row by about 3/4 inch (1.8 cm).

Free-view the rows. What do you see? You may need to adjust the distances between the coins a little in order to create the best "pop" for your money.

Once you have created the effect with same-sized coins, try using different-sized coins for different rows. How might this affect the illusion? To get the best illusion, should larger coins be placed closer or farther apart?

What happens:

When you free-view the row of coins, the coins overlap. The top row, where the coins are the closest together, appears to float higher, above the other coins. The bottom row of coins appears to be farthest away. The middle row of coins floats between the two rows.

Why:

The wallpaper effect is another example of overlapping images to create a three-dimensional illusion. Unlike image pairs, the wallpaper illusion uses a repeating pattern of subjects for overlapping.

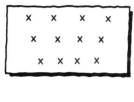

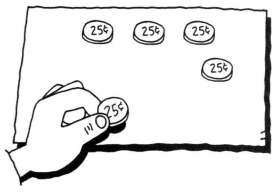

Seeing Red . . . and Blue

You've seen them before—those red/blue eyeglasses that make certain pictures look like they're jumping out at you. There's a good chance you have a pair lying around in some pile of junk or tucked away in a lost comic book. In this experiment, you'll make your own.

You need:

light red and light blue pencils
red and blue scraps of see-through
    plastic (from report covers or
    old lighting gels)
white paper

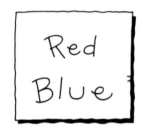

What to do:

Use your red pencil to write the word "red" in the middle of a sheet of paper. Just beneath this word, use the blue pencil to write the word "blue."

Close one eye and look through the piece of blue plastic with your other eye. Which word appears darker? Does one word disappear?

If the word "blue" doesn't fade when you look through the blue plastic, try using a different shade of blue plastic. If that doesn't work, try doubling the thickness of the plastic or try using a different shade of blue pencil.

Put the blue plastic down. Close one eye and look through the red plastic. Which word appears darkest now? Does the red disappear? If it doesn't, try using a different shade of red plastic, doubling the thickness of the plastic, or using a different shade of red pencil.

Once you've got it, hold the blue plastic to one eye and the red plastic to the other eye. With both eyes open, look at the words. Weird, huh? Close one eye. Then close the other. What happens to the words?

What happens:

When you look through the blue plastic, everything gets tinted blue. This makes the blue pencil marks fade into the blue-tinted background and disappear. At the same time, the blue tint makes the red pencil marks look darker and stand out.

When you look through the red plastic, everything gets tinted red. This makes the red pencil marks fade into the red-tinted background and disappear. At the same time, the red tint makes the blue pencil marks look darker and stand out.

Why:

The red plastic acts as a filter to cut out blue light and make the printed blue lines appear black. Likewise, the blue plastic acts as a filter to cut out the red light and make the printed red lines appear black. When you switch eyes, you see only the blackened lines, making the scene appear to jump. When you look with both eyes, you see a red and blue mixed-up view.

Making Targets

By themselves, the red and blue filters can't make things appear in three dimensions. There is nothing magical about those two colors together. In order for the filters to create the illusion of depth, they need to be used with special images. These images are drawings or photographs that have both red and blue lines.

You need:
  light red and light blue pencils
  red and blue scraps of see-through plastic
  paper
  NOTE: In order to do this experiment, the pencils and filters must work from the last experiment, Seeing Red ... and Blue (pages 116-117).

What to do:
Use your red pencil to draw a column of three small-coin circles.

Use your blue pencil to add three circles of the same size. Look at the drawing to see where these blue circles need to be drawn. The top blue circle should be slightly to the right of the red circle so that the red and blue lines appear side by side. The middle blue circle needs to be about 1/8 inch (.3 cm) to the right of the middle red circle. The bottom blue circle should be about 1/3 inch (.9 cm) to the right of the bottom red circle.

Place the blue filter over one eye and the red filter over the other. Look at these pairs of circles. What do you see? Do they all appear at the same height or do some appear to float above others? Can you see how the distance between the red and blue circles compares to the height that each image rises?

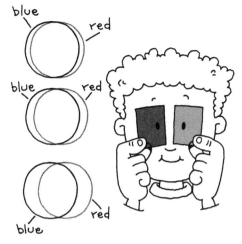

What do you think will happen to the illusion when you switch filters? After you've guessed, try it and find out. How does switching the red and blue filters affect the illusion?

What happens:

Your brain brings together the red and blue images and creates the illusion of circles coming toward or moving away from you.

Why:

Images made of red and blue parts are called *anaglyphs*. Each of the anaglyph pair of circles that you drew has a different distance between the blue and red circle. The anaglyph with the greatest distance between the blue and red circle creates the strongest three-dimensional effect. Its circle appears to either come closest or move farthest away from you. Whether it moves toward you or away depends on which filter is over which eye.

A Smooth Transition

The circles that you created in the last experiment are excellent subjects for showing how depth jumps back and forth. But did you know that you can just as easily create a smooth change in depth?

You need:

light red and light blue pencils

paper

ruler

red and blue scraps of see-through plastic

NOTE: In order to do this experiment, the pencils and filters must work from the experiment called Seeing Red ... and Blue (see pages 116-117).

What to do:

Use your ruler to draw the two lines shown on the opposite pages. Draw one line red. Draw the other one blue.

Before looking at these with your red and blue filters, guess what the illusion will look like. Which end of the line will appear to come toward or away from you?

Now use your red and blue filters to look at these two lines. What do you see?

How can you make the illusion stronger? How far can you separate the lines?

Suppose you made an "X" by crossing a blue and red line. How might that illusion appear? Make a guess. Then try it and find out.

What happens:

The separate red and blue lines come together into a single line. The top of the line appears to be on the page. The other end (depending on which filter is on which eye) is floating either above or below the page.

Why:

Your brain brings the two separated lines into a single image that has depth. Since the distance between the two lines increases gradually, your brain makes an illusion in which the line smoothly and evenly bends away from the paper.

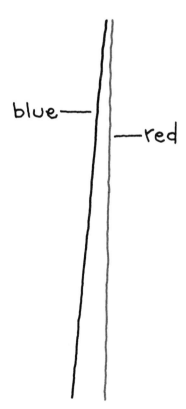

blue—   —red

3-D Cube

As you've probably guessed, the red and blue lines of anaglyphs represent right-eye and left-eye views (or left-eye and right-eye views, depending upon which color is where). Unlike side-by-side stereoimages, the different images of an anaglyph are "stamped" one on top of the other. The result looks like a double-exposure mess!

However, the red and blue filters separate the anaglyph into their own right-eye and left-eye images. Your brain does the rest and uses the slight difference in appearance to make the scene three-dimensional.

You need:
> light red and light blue pencils
> pencil with eraser
> red and blue scraps of see-through plastic
> white paper

NOTE: In order to do this experiment, the pencils and filters must work from the earlier experiment, Seeing Red . . . and Blue (see pages 116–117).

What to do:
Place the blank white paper over the stencil marked "red cube." Use your red pencil to trace the lines of the cube. Use a regular pencil to make a light mark on the crosshair where shown. This mark will be used to line up the two stencils.

Once the red cube is complete, move on to the blue cube. Carefully position your page on top of the stencil marked "blue cube" so that the crosshairs line up. Now use your blue pencil to trace the lines of this slightly different cube.

When the blue outline is complete, place your page on top of a flat desk. Carefully erase the crosshair.

Place the blue filter over one eye and the red filter over the other. Look at the cube anaglyph. What do you see? Do any parts of the cube appear to "pop" out? Switch the viewing filters. How does this affect the illusion?

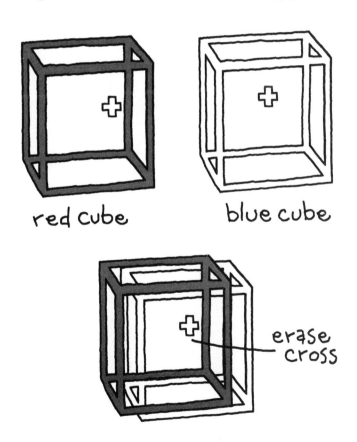

red cube   blue cube

erase cross

What happens:
Your brain brings the red and blue outlines together and makes the illusion of a three-dimensional cube.

Why:
It's the same story of looking at something from different views. Although the anaglyph looks like a printing mistake, it actually has two slightly different and overlapping images. The colored filters separate the images and send one to each eye. Your brain does the rest. Using the difference in the image appearance, it makes the illusion of a three-dimensional cube.

INDEX

Afterimage, 56–59
  defined, 57
  experiments, 56–59
Anaglyphs, 119, 122–124
Arch illusion, 92–93
Arrowheads, 76
Binocular vision, 103,
  104–105
Bird-flight experiments,
  24–25, 26–27
Brain
  constant comparisons of,
    82, 97
  filling in "in-between"
    action, 28–30
  interpreting TV shows, 8–9
  length/size illusions and,
    66–67. *See also* Distortions
    (length and size)
  optic nerve and, 43
  overlapping images, 99,
    102, 105, 106, 110, 113,
    114–115
  overload, compensation for,
    8–9
  reference book in, 66–67
  rules of, 67, 73, 91
  shortcuts in, 6, 8–9
Candle experiment, 18–19
Coin illusions, 79–82

Color illusions
  Balancing Act, 60–61
  Color Code, 56–57
  Colors in Black and White,
    64–65
  Comparing Colors, 96–97
  A Different Spin on Color
    Perception, 62–63
  Making Targets, 118–119
  Pink Pigs, 58–59
  Seeing Red...and Blue,
    116–117
  Setting a Side Aside, 95
  A Smooth Transition, 120–121
  3-D Cube, 122–124
  Where Did You Get Those
    Shades?, 48
  Where Have All the Colors
    Gone?, 46–47
Colors
  afterimages of, 56–59
  anaglyphs and, 119, 122–124
  blending into white, 62–63
  in bright vs. dark light,
    46–47, 48, 50
  comparing, 96–97
  complementary, 57, 61
  filtering, experiments, 116–124
  imaginary (Fechner lines),
    64–65

Colors (*cont*)
  losing sensitivity to, 47, 61
  shades of, 48, 52–53
  visual color-correction system, 60–61
  visual purple and, 55
Distortions (length and size), 66–84
  Adding Arrowheads, 76
  Coining an Illusion, 79–80
  Illusionary Lengths, 68–71
  More Coinage, 81–82
  Müller-Lyer illusion and, 76, 77–78, 80
  overview, 66–67
  Room for Mistakes, 72–73
  Rulers Don't Lie...Right?, 77–78
  Tracks of the Trade, 74–75
  Tricky Trapezoids, 83–84
Distortions, other. *See* Tilts, twists, and topsy-turvies
Eye
  afterimages, defined, 57
  blind spot, 44–45
  cornea, 42
  dominant and recessive, 104–105
  floaters in, 51
  fovea, 43, 50, 53
  how it works, 42–43
  illustrated, 43
  iris, 43

  jelly-like stuff inside, 51
  lens, 43
  optic nerve and, 5, 43, 45, 66
  parts of, 42–43
  pupil, 42–43
  retina, 43, 45, 50, 55, 102
  rods and cones, 43, 45, 47, 48, 50, 53, 65
  seeing different images in each, 105, 107. *See also* Illusions of depth
  visual purple in, 55
Eye tricks, 42–65
  Balancing Act, 60–61
  Blind Spot, 44–45
  Color Code, 56–57
  Colors in Black and White, 64–65
  A Different Spin on Color Perception, 62–63
  Field Trip, 49–50
  More Fieldwork, 51
  Not Fade Away, 54–55
  Pink Pigs, 58–59
  Pump Up the Difference, 52–53
  Where Did You Get Those Shades?, 48
  Where Have All the Colors Gone?, 46–47
Fechner lines, 64–65
Fish flip books, 32–33, 39–41

Flip book experiments
    A Cast of Two, 39–41
    Flippin' Fin Fun, 32–33
    overview, 31
    Stencil the Snail, 34–36
    Twists and Turns, 37–38
Fly flip book, 37–38
Frames
    flip book experiments, 31, 32–41
    key, experiments with, 24–30
    in movie films, 9
Free viewing, experiments with, 111–115
Frog-spinner experiment, 21–23
Hardwired illusions. *See* Eye tricks
Illusions of depth, 102–124
    Come Together, 105–106
    Dominant View, 104–105
    Free Viewing, 111–112
    Handy Hold-in-One, 106–107
    Making Targets, 118–119
    overlapping images and, 102, 105, 106, 110, 113, 114–115
    overview, 102–103
    Seeing Red...and Blue, 116–117
    A Smooth Transition, 120–121
    Stereo Pairs, 108–110
    3-D Cube, 122–124
    Two-Level Float, 113

Wallpaper, 114–115
Illusions of motion, 8–41
    Beamer, 16–17
    brain shortcuts and, 6, 8–9
    Fan Trails, 14–15
    Flappin' Without a Flipper, 26–27
    Flights of Imagination, 24–25
    Happy Trails, 12–13
    Lasting Thoughts, 10–11
    Light the Candle, 18–19
    Shoebox Spinner, 21–23
    Slot Shot, 28–30
In-between action, 28–30
Inward-bending square, 88
Key frame experiments
    Flappin' Without a Flipper, 26–27
    Flights of Imagination, 24–25
    key frame defined, 25
    Slot Shot, 28–30
Landscape orientation, 68
Length illusions. *See* Distortions (length and size)
Light show experiment, 12–13
Mosaic illusion, 100–101
Motion illusions. *See* Illusions of motion
Müller-Lyer illusion, 76, 77–78, 80
Optical illusions. *See also* specific types of illusions
    brain shortcuts and, 6, 8–9

Optical illusions (*cont*)
    perception and, 5–6
    source of, 5–6
    unknown explanations of, 85
    watching TV and, 8–9
Overlap, 99, 102, 105, 106,
    110, 113, 114–115
Parallel lines illusion, 86–87
Persistence of vision
    experiments, 10–11, 16–18,
    32–38
Railroad tracks illusion, 74–75
Rulers, illusions with, 77–78,
    94
Safety precautions, 7
Shark flip book, 32–33
Size illusions. *See* Distortions
    (length and size)
Snail flip book, 34–36
Spinning experiments, 18–23
Stars/planets, brightness of,
    49–50
Thaumatrope (spinning
    marvels), 18–23
Three dimensions. *See also*
    Illusions of depth
    binocular vision and, 103,
        104–105
    explaining illusions, 71,
        73, 75, 76, 89
    overlap and, 102
    seeing, factors influencing,
        102–103

Tilts, twists, and topsy-turvies,
    85–101
    Arch Enemy, 92–93
    Bending In, 88
    Comparing Colors, 96–97
    Imaginary Square, 98
    Mosaic Madness, 100–101
    A New Slant on Things,
      86–87
    Ruler Interference, 94
    Setting a Side Aside, 95
    unknown explanations
      and, 85–101
    Upside Downside, 90–91
    Warp Speed, 89
Trapezoid trick, 83–84
TV, brain interpreting, 8–9
Unstable figures, 95
Upside-down illusion, 90–91
Vision. *See also* Eye; Eye tricks
    binocular, 103, 104–105
    color and. *See* Color
      illusions; Colors
    experience influencing, 5
    persistence of, experiments,
      10–11, 16–18, 32–38
    source of optical illusions,
      5–6
    understanding what you
      see, 5–6
Visual fields, exploring, 49–50
Wallpaper effect, 114–115